CW00403635

My Adventure

Baden-Powell of Gilwell

Alpha Editions

Copyright © 2018

ISBN : 9789352977116

Design and Setting By
Alpha Editions
email - alphaedis@gmail.com

All rights reserved. No part of this publication may be
reproduced, distributed, or transmitted in any form or by
means, including photocopying, recording, or other
electronic or mechanical methods, without the prior
written permission of the publisher.

The views and characters expressed in the book are of the
author and his/her imagination and do not represent the
views of the Publisher.

Contents

MY ADVENTURES AS A SPY

It has been difficult to write in peace-time on the delicate subject of spies and spying, but now that the war is in progress and the methods of those much abused gentry have been disclosed, there is no harm in going more fully into the question, and to relate some of my own personal experiences.

Spies are like ghosts—people seem to have had a general feeling that there might be such things, but they did not at the same time believe in them—because they never saw them, and seldom met anyone who had had first-hand experience of them. But as regards the spies, I can speak with personal knowledge in saying that they do exist, and in very large numbers, not only in England, but in every part of Europe.

As in the case of ghosts, any phenomenon which people don't understand, from a sudden crash on a quiet day to a midnight creak of a cupboard, has an affect of alarm upon nervous minds. So also a spy is spoken of with undue alarm and abhorrence, because he is somewhat of a bogey.

As a first step it is well to disabuse one's mind of the idea that every spy is necessarily the base and despicable fellow he is generally held to be. He is often both clever and brave.

The term "spy" is used rather indiscriminately, and has by use come to be a term of contempt. As a misapplication of the term "spy" the case of Major André always seems to me to have been rather a hard one. He was a Swiss by birth, and during the American War of Independence in 1780 joined the British Army in Canada, where he ultimately became A.D.C. to General Sir H. Clinton.

The American commander of a fort near West Point, on the Hudson River, had hinted that he wanted to surrender, and Sir H. Clinton sent André to treat with him. In order to get through the American lines André dressed himself in plain clothes and took the name of John Anderson. He was unfortunately caught by the Americans and tried by court martial and hanged as a spy.

As he was not trying to get information, it seems scarcely right to call him a spy. Many people took this view at the time, and George III. gave his mother a pension, as well as a title to his brother, and his body was ultimately dug up and re-interred in Westminster Abbey.

THE DIFFERENT DEGREES OF SPIES

Let us for the moment change the term "spy" to "investigator" or "military agent." For war purposes these agents may be divided into:

1. *Strategical* and diplomatic *agents*, who study the political and military conditions in peace time of all other countries which might eventually be in opposition to their own in war. These also create political disaffection and organise outbreaks, such, for instance, as spreading sedition amongst Egyptians, or in India amongst the inhabitants, or in South Africa amongst the Boer population, to bring about an outbreak, if possible, in order to create confusion and draw off troops in time of war.

2. *Tactical*, military, or naval *agents*, who look into minor details of armament and terrain in peace time. These also make tactical preparations on the spot, such as material for extra bridges, gun emplacements, interruption of communications, etc.

3. *Field spies*. Those who act as scouts in disguise to reconnoitre positions and to report moves of the enemy in the field of war. Amongst these are residential spies and officer agents.

All these duties are again subdivided among agents of every grade, from ambassadors and their attachés downwards. Naval and military officers are sent to carry out special investigations by all countries, and paid detectives are stationed in likely centres to gather information.

There are also traitor spies. For these I allow I have not a good word. They are men who sell their countries' secrets for money. Fortunately we are not much troubled with them in England; but we have had a notorious example in South Africa.

STRATEGICAL AGENTS

The war treason—that is, preliminary political and strategical investigation—of the Germans in the present campaign has not been such a success as might have been expected from a scheme so wonderfully organised as it has been. With the vast sums spent upon it, the German General Staff might reasonably have obtained men in a higher position in life who could have gauged the political atmosphere better than was done by their agents immediately before the present crisis.

Their plans for starting strikes at a critical time met with no response whatever. They had great ideas of stirring up strife and discontent among the Mahommedan populations both in Egypt and in India, but they calculated without knowing enough of the Eastern races or their feelings towards Great Britain and Germany—more especially Germany.

They looked upon the Irish question as being a certainty for civil war in Britain, and one which would necessitate the employment of a large proportion of our expeditionary force within our own islands.

They never foresaw that the Boer and Briton would be working amicably in South Africa; they had supposed that the army of occupation there could never be removed, and did not foresee that South Africa would be sending a contingent against their South African colonies while the regulars came to strengthen our army at home.

They imagined the Overseas Dominions were too weak in men and ships and training to be of any use; and they never foresaw that the manhood of Great Britain would come forward in vast numbers to take up arms for which their national character has to a large extent given them the necessary qualifications. All this might have been discovered if the Germans had employed men of a higher education and social position.

TACTICAL AGENTS

In addition to finding out military details about a country, such as its preparedness in men, supplies, efficiency, and so on, these agents have to study the tactical features of hills and plains, roads and railways, rivers and woods, and even the probable battlefields and their artillery positions, and so on.

The Germans in the present war have been using the huge guns whose shells, owing to their black, smoky explosions, have been nicknamed "Black Marias" or "Jack Johnsons." These guns require strong concrete foundations for them to stand upon before they can be fired. But the Germans foresaw this long before the war, and laid their plans accordingly.

They examined all the country over which they were likely to fight, both in Belgium and in France, and wherever they saw good positions for guns they built foundations and emplacements for them. This was done in the time of peace, and therefore had to be done secretly. In order to divert suspicion, a German would buy or rent a farm on which it was desired to build an emplacement. Then he would put down foundations for a new barn or farm building, or—if near a town—for a factory, and when these were complete, he would erect some lightly constructed building upon it.

There was nothing to attract attention or suspicion about this, and numbers of these emplacements are said to have been made before war began. When war broke out and the troops arrived on the ground, the buildings were hastily pulled down and there were the emplacements all ready for the guns.

Some years ago a report came to the War Office that a foreign Power was making gun emplacements in a position which had not before been suspected of being of military value, and they were evidently going to use it for strategical purposes.

I was sent to see whether the report was true. Of course, it would not do to go as an officer—suspicions would be aroused, one would be allowed to see nothing, and would probably be arrested as a spy. I therefore went to stay with a friendly farmer in the neighbourhood, and went out shooting every day among the partridges and snipe which abounded there. The first thing I did was to look at the country generally, and try to think which points would be most valuable as positions for artillery.

Then I went to look for partridges (and other things!) on the hills which I had noticed, and I very soon found what I wanted.

Officers were there, taking angles and measurements, accompanied by workmen, who were driving pegs into the ground and marking off lines with tapes between them.

As I passed with my gun in my hand, bag on shoulder, and dog at heel, they paid no attention to me, and from the neighbouring hills I was able to watch their proceedings.

When they went away to their meals or returned to their quarters, I went shooting over the ground they had left, and if I did not get a big bag of game, at any rate I made a good collection of drawings and measurements of the plans of the forts and emplacements which they had traced out on the ground.

So that within a few days of their starting to make them we had the plans of them all in our possession. Although they afterwards planted trees all over the sites to conceal the forts within them, and put up buildings in other places to hide them, we knew perfectly well where the emplacements were and what were their shapes and sizes.

This planting of trees to hide such defence works occasionally has the other effect, and shows one where they are. This was notably the case at Tsingtau, captured by the Japanese and British forces from the Germans. As there were not any natural woods there, I had little difficulty in finding where the forts were by reason of the plantations of recent growth in the neighbourhood of the place.

RESIDENTIAL SPIES

These men take up their quarters more or less permanently in the country of their operations. A few are men in high places in the social or commercial world, and are generally *nouveaux riches*, anxious for decorations and rewards. But most of the residential spies are of a more insignificant class, and in regular pay for their work.

Their duty is to act as agents to receive and distribute instructions secretly to other itinerant spies, and to return their reports to headquarters. For this reason they are nicknamed in the German Intelligence Bureau "post-boxes." They also themselves pick up what information they can from all available sources and transmit it home.

One, Steinbauer, has for some years past been one of the principal "post-boxes" in England. He was attached to the Kaiser's staff during his last visit to this country, when he came as the guest of the King to the opening of Queen Victoria's memorial.

A case of espionage which was tried in London revealed his methods, one of his agents being arrested after having been watched for three years.

Karl Ernst's trial confirmed the discoveries and showed up the doings of men spies like Schroeder, Gressa, Klare, and others.

Also the case of Dr. Karl Graves may be still in the memory of many. This German was arrested in Scotland for spying, and was condemned to eighteen months' imprisonment, and was shortly afterwards released without any reason being officially assigned. He has since written a full account of what he did, and it is of interest to note how his correspondence passed to and from the intelligence headquarters in Germany in envelopes embellished with the name of Messrs. Burroughs and Wellcome, the famous chemists. He posed as a doctor, and sent his letters through an innkeeper at Brussels or a *modiste* in Paris, while letters to him came through an obscure tobacconist's shop in London.

One of these letters miscarried through having the wrong initial to his name. It was returned by the Post Office to Burroughs and Wellcome, who on opening it found inside a German letter, enclosing bank-notes in return for services rendered. This raised suspicion against him. He was watched, and finally arrested.

He states that a feeling that he was being followed dawned upon him one day, when he noticed in his lodgings that the clothes which he had folded on a chair had been since refolded in a slightly different way while he was out. With some suspicion, he asked his landlady whether anyone had entered his room, and she, in evident confusion, denied that any stranger could have been there. Then he suggested that his tailor might have called, and she agreed that it was so. But when an hour or two later he interviewed his tailor, he, on his part, said he had not been near the place. Graves consequently deduced that he was being followed.

The knowledge that you are being watched, and you don't know by whom, gives, I can assure you, a very jumpy feeling—especially when you know you are guilty.

I can speak feelingly from more than one experience of it, since I have myself been employed on this form of scouting in peace time.

OFFICER AGENTS

It is generally difficult to find ordinary spies who are also sufficiently imbued with technical knowledge to be of use in gaining naval or military details. Consequently officers are often employed to obtain such information in peace time as well as in the theatre of action in war.

But with them, and especially with those of Germany, it is not easy to find men who are sufficiently good actors, or who can disguise their appearance so well as to evade suspicion. Very many of these have visited our shores during the past few years, but they have generally been noticed, watched, and followed, and from the line taken by them in their reconnaissance it has been easy to deduce the kind of operations contemplated in their plans.

I remember the case of a party of these motoring through Kent nominally looking at old Roman ruins. When they asked a landowner for the exact position of some of these he regretted he had not a map handy on which he could point out their position. One of the "antiquarians" at once produced a large scale map; but it was not an English map: it had, for instance, details on it regarding water supply tanks which, though they existed, were not shown on any of our ordnance maps!

In addition to the various branches of spying which I have mentioned, the Germans have also practised commercial espionage on systematic lines.

COMMERCIAL SPYING

Young Germans have been often known to serve in British business houses without salary in order to "learn the language"; they took care to learn a good deal more than the language, and picked up many other things about trade methods and secrets which were promptly utilised in their own country. The importance of commercial spying is that commercial war is all the time at the bottom of Germany's preparations for military war.

Carl Lody, a German ex-officer, was recently tried in London by court-martial and shot for "war treason"—that is, for sending information regarding our Navy to Germany during hostilities. ("War treason" is secret work outside the zone of war operations. When carried on within the zone of operations it is called spying or "espionage.") Carl Lody's moves were watched and his correspondence opened by the counter-spy police in London, and thus all his investigations and information were known to the War Office long before he was arrested.

The enormous sums paid by Germany for many years past have brought about a sort of international spy exchange, generally formed of American-Germans, with their headquarters in Belgium, and good prices were given for information acquired by them. For instance, if the plans of a new fort, or the dimensions of a new ship, or the power of a new gun were needed, one merely had to apply and state a price to this bureau to receive fairly good information on the subject before much time had elapsed.

At the same time, by pretending to be an American, one was able to get a good deal of minor and useful information without the expenditure of a cent.

GERMANY'S INVASION PLANS

On getting into touch with these gentry, I was informed of one of the intended plans by which the Germans proposed to invade our country, and incidentally it throws some light on their present methods of dealing with the inhabitants as apart from the actual tactical movements of the troops.

The German idea then—some six years ago—was that they could, by means of mines and submarines, at any time block the traffic in the British Channel in the space of a few hours, thus holding our home fleets in their stations at Spithead and Portland.

With the Straits of Dover so blocked, they could then rush a fleet of transports across the North Sea from Germany, to the East Coast of England, either East Anglia or, as in this plan, in Yorkshire. They had in Germany nine embarking stations, with piers and platforms, all ready made, and steel lighters for disembarkation purposes or for actual traversing of the ocean in case of fine weather.

They had taken the average of the weather for years past, and had come to the conclusion that July 13th is, on an average, the finest day in the year; but their attempt would be timed, if possible, to fall on a Bank Holiday when communications were temporarily disorganised. Therefore the nearest Bank Holiday to July 13th would probably be that at the beginning of August; it was a coincidence that the present war broke out on that day.

The spies stationed in England were to cut all telephone and telegraph wires, and, where possible, to blow down important bridges and tunnels, and thus to interrupt communications and create confusion.

Their idea of landing on the coast of Yorkshire was based on the following reasons:—

They do not look upon London as strategically the capital of England, but rather upon the great industrial centres of the north Midlands, where, instead of six millions, there are more like fourteen millions of people assembled in the numerous cities and towns, which now almost adjoin each other across that part of the country.

Their theory was that if they could rush an army of even 90,000 men into Leeds, Sheffield, Halifax, Manchester, and Liverpool without encountering great opposition in the first few hours, they could there establish themselves in such strength that it would require a powerful army to drive them out again.

Bringing a week's provisions with them, and seizing all the local provisions, they would have enough to sustain them for a considerable time, and the first step of their occupation would be to expel every inhabitant—man, woman, and child—from the neighbourhood and destroy the towns. Thus, within a few hours, some fourteen millions of people would be starving, and wandering without shelter over the face of the country—a disaster which would need a large force to deal with, and would cause entire disruption of our food supplies and of business in the country.

The East Coast of Yorkshire between the Humber and Scarborough lends itself to such an adventure, by providing a good open beach for miles, with open country in front of it, which, in its turn, is protected by a semi-circle of wolds, which could be easily held by the German covering force. Its left would be protected by the Humber and the right by the Tees, so that the landing could be carried out without interruption.

That was their plan—based on careful investigation by a small army of spies—some five or six years ago, before our naval bases had been established in the north. If they had declared war then, they, might have had no serious interference from our Navy during the passage of their transports, which, of course, would be protected on that flank by their entire fleet of warships.

At first glance, it seems too fanciful a plan to commend itself to belief, but in talking it over with German officers, I found they fully believed in it as a practical proposition. They themselves enlarged on the idea of the use that they would thus make of the civil population, and foreshadowed their present brutality by explaining that when war came, it would not be made with kid gloves. The meaning of their commands would be brought home to the people by shooting down civilians if necessary, in order to prove that they were in earnest, and to force the inhabitants through terror to comply with their requirements.

Further investigations on the subject proved that the embarkation arrangements were all planned and prepared for. At any time in the ordinary way of commerce there were numerous large mail steamers always available in their ports to transport numbers even largely in excess of those that would be assembled for such an expedition. Troops could be mobilised in the neighbourhood of the ports, ostensibly for manoeuvres, without suspicion being aroused.

It is laid down in German strategical textbooks that the time for making war is not when you have a political cause for it, but when your troops are ready and the enemy is unready; and that to strike the first blow is the best way to declare war.

I recounted all this at the time in a private lecture to officers, illustrated with lantern slides and maps, as a military problem which would be interesting to work out on the actual ground, and it was not really until the report of this leaked into the papers that I realised how nearly I had "touched the spot." For, apart from the various indignant questions with which the Secretary of State for War was badgered in the House of Commons on my account, I was assailed with letters from Germany of most violent abuse from various quarters, high and low, which showed me that I had gone nearer the truth than I had even suspected.

"You are but a brown-paper general," said one, "and if you think that by your foolish talk you are to frighten us from coming, you are not right."

FIELD SPIES

It is difficult to say where exactly a spy's work ends in war, and that of a scout begins, except that, as a rule, the first is carried out in disguise.

The scout is looked up to as a brave man, and his expedients for gaining information are thought wonderfully clever, so long as he remains in uniform. If he goes a bit further, and finds that he can get his information better by adopting a disguise—even at the greater risk to himself through the certainty of being shot if he is found out—then he is looked down upon as a "despicable spy." I don't see the justice of it myself.

A good spy—no matter which country he serves—is *of necessity* a brave and valuable fellow.

In our Army we do not make a very wide use of field spies on service, though their partial use at manoeuvres has shown what they can do.

In "Aids to Scouting" I have stated: "In the matter of spying we are behind other nations. Spying, in reality, is reconnaissance in disguise. Its effects are so far-reaching that most nations, in order to deter enemies' spies, threaten them with death if caught."

As an essential part of scouting, I gave a chapter of hints on how to spy, and how to catch other people spying.

CATCHING A SPY

Spy-catching was once one of my duties, and is perhaps the best form of education towards successful spying. I had been lucky enough to nail three and was complimented by one of the senior officers on the Commander-in-Chief's staff. We were riding home together from a big review at the time that he was talking about it, and he remarked, "How do you set about catching a spy?" I told him of our methods and added that also luck very often came in and helped one.

Just in front of us, in the crowd of vehicles returning from the review-ground, was an open hired Victoria in which sat a foreign-looking gentleman. I remarked that as an instance this was the sort of man I should keep an eye upon, and I should quietly follow him till I found where he lodged and then put a detective on to report his moves.

From our position on horseback close behind him we were able to see that our foreigner was reading a guide book and was studying a map of the fortifications through which we were passing. Suddenly he called to the driver to stop for a moment while he lit a match for his cigarette. The driver pulled up, and so did we. The stranger glanced up to see that the man was not looking round, and then quickly slipped a camera from under the rug which was lying on the seat in front of him, and taking aim at the entrance shaft of a new ammunition store which had just been made for our Navy, he took a snapshot.

Then hurriedly covering up the camera again he proceeded to strike matches and to light his cigarette. Then he gave the word to drive on again.

We followed close behind till we came to where a policeman was regulating the traffic. I rode ahead and gave him his instructions so that the carriage was stopped, and the man was asked to show his permit to take photographs. He had none. The camera was taken into custody and the name and address of the owner taken "with a view to further proceedings."

Unfortunately at that time—it was many years ago—we were badly handicapped by our laws in the matter of arresting and punishing spies. By-laws allowed us to confiscate and smash unauthorised cameras, and that was all.

"Further proceedings," had they been possible, in this case would have been unnecessary, for the suspected gentleman took himself off to the Continent by the very next boat.

But it took a good deal to persuade my staff-officer friend that the whole episode was not one faked up for his special edification.

It is only human to hate to be outwitted by one more clever than yourself, and perhaps that accounts for people disliking spies with a more deadly hatred than that which they bestow on a man who drops bombs from an aeroplane indiscriminately on women and children, or who bombards cathedrals with infernal engines of war.

Nobody could say that my native spy in South Africa, Jan Grootboom, was either a contemptible or mean kind of man. He was described by one who knew him as a "white man in a black skin," and I heartily endorse the description.

Here is an instance of his work as a field spy:—

Jan Grootboom was a Zulu by birth, but having lived much with white men, as a hunter and guide, he had taken to wearing ordinary clothes and spoke English perfectly well: but within him he had all the pluck and cunning of his race.

For scouting against the Matabele it was never wise to take a large party, since it would be sure to attract attention, whereas by going alone with one man, such as Grootboom, one was able to penetrate their lines and to lie hid almost among them, watching their disposition and gaining information as to their numbers, supplies, and whereabouts of their women and cattle, etc.

Now, every night was spent at this work—that is to say, the night was utilised for creeping to their positions, and one watched them during the day. But it was impossible to do this without leaving footmarks and tracks, which the sharp eyes of their scouts were not slow to discover, and it very soon dawned upon them that they were being watched, and consequently they were continually on the look-out to waylay and capture us.

One night Grootboom and I had ridden to the neighbourhood of one of the enemy's camps, and were lying waiting for the early dawn before we could discover exactly where they were located.

It was during the hour before sunrise that, as a rule, the enemy used to light their fires for cooking their early morning food. One could thus see exactly their position, and could rectify one's own, so as to find a place where one could lie by during the day and watch their movements.

On this occasion the first fire was lit and then another sparkled up, and yet another, but before half a dozen had been lighted Grootboom suddenly growled under his breath:—

"The swine—they are laying a trap for us."

I did not understand at the moment what he meant, but he said:—

"Stop here for a bit, and I will go and look."

He slipped off all his clothing and left it lying in a heap, and stole away in the darkness, practically naked. Evidently he was going to visit them to see what was going on.

The worst of spying is that it makes you always suspicious, even of your best friends. So, as soon as Grootboom was gone in one direction, I quietly crept away in another, and got among some rocks in a small kopje, where I should have some kind of a chance if he had any intention of betraying me and returning with a few Matabele to capture me.

For an hour or two I lay there, until presently I saw Grootboom creeping back through the grass—alone.

Ashamed of my doubts, I therefore came out and went to our rendezvous, and found him grinning all over with satisfaction while he was putting on his clothes again. He said that he had found as he had expected, an ambush laid for us. The thing that had made him suspicious was that the fires, instead of lighting up all over the hillside at different points about the same time, had been lighted in steady succession one after another, evidently by one man going round. This struck him as suspicious, and he then assumed that it was done to lead us on, if we were anywhere around, to go and examine more closely the locality.

He had crept in towards them by a devious path, from which he was able to perceive a whole party of the Matabele lying low in the grass by the track which we should probably have used in getting there, and they would have pounced upon us and captured us.

To make sure of this suspicion he crept round till near their stronghold, and coming from there he got in among them and chatted away with them, finding out what was their intention with regard to ourselves, and also what were their plans for the near future. Then, having left them, and walked boldly back towards their stronghold, he crept away amongst some rocks and rejoined me.

His was an example of the work of a field spy which, although in a way it may be cunning and deceitful, at the same time demands the greatest personal courage and astuteness. It is something greater than the ordinary bravery of a soldier in action, who is carried on by the enthusiasm of those around him under the leadership of an officer, and with the competition and admiration of others.

The pluck of the man who goes out alone, unobserved and unapplauded, and at the risk of his life, is surely equally great.

The Boers used field spies freely against us in South Africa.

One English-speaking Boer used to boast how, during the war, he made frequent visits to Johannesburg dressed in the uniform taken from a British major who had been killed in action. He used to ride past the sentries, who, instead of shooting him, merely saluted, and he frequented the clubs and other resorts of the officers, picking up such information as he required from them first hand, till evening came and he was able to ride back to his commando.

CONVEYING INFORMATION

On our side various methods were adopted of conveying information in the field. My spies employed native runners (especially the most astute cattle-thieves) to take their despatches to me.

A SECRET MESSAGE.

These hieroglyphics contain a secret message which can be easily read by those who know the semaphore signalling code. This signalling consists of swinging two arms in different positions, either singly or together. The dots indicate where the letters join. For example: The semaphore sign for N consists of both arms pointing downwards at an angle of 90 degrees ^. The letter I is shown by both arms pointing to the left at the same angle >. The next N is shown again, and the letter E is a single arm pointing upwards on the right at an angle of 45 degrees /.

In each word you start at the top of the signs and read downwards.

This form of secret message was frequently used in the South African War.

These were in every case naturally written in cypher or secret code, in Hindustani written in English characters, and so on. They were rolled up into pellets and pressed into a small hole bored in a walking-stick, the hole being then plugged with clay or soap. Or they were put into the bowl of a pipe underneath the

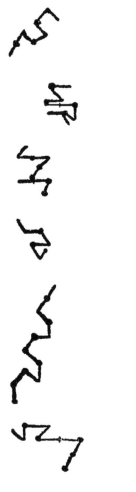

N
I
N
E

F
O
R
T
S

W
H
E
R
E

Y
O
U

E
X
P
E
C
T
E
D

T
H
R
E
E

tobacco, and could thus be burnt without suspicion if necessary, or they were slipped in between the soles of the boots, or stitched in the lining of the bearer's clothing. These natives also understood the language of smoke-fires—signalling by means of little or big puffs of smoke as to the enemy's moves and strength.

SECRET SIGNALS AND WARNINGS

The native despatch-runners whom we sent out to make their way through the enemy's lines carried the letters tightly rolled up in little balls, coated with sheet lead, such as tea is packed in.

These little balls they carried slung round their necks on a string. The moment that they saw an enemy coming near they dropped the balls, which then looked like so many stones, on the ground, and took bearings of the spot so that they could find them again when the coast was clear.

Then there were fixed points for hiding letters for other spies to find. Here are some of the most frequently used:

This little mark, scratched on the ground or on a tree trunk or gate-post, was used by one scout for the information of another. It means: "A letter is hidden four paces in this direction."

A sign used to warn another scout that he is following a wrong direction. It means: "Not this way."

This is another sign from one scout to another and means: "I have returned home."

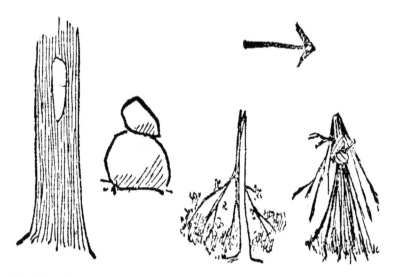

The "blaze" on the tree trunk and the two stones, one on the other, are simply to show that the scout is on the right trail.

The other three sketches are to show the direction in which the scout should go. The arrow is marked on the ground. The upper part of the sapling or bush is bent over in the direction which the scout should take, and the same is the case with the bunch of grass, which is first of all knotted and then bent.

SPIES IN WAR TIME

The Japanese, of course, in their war with Russia in Manchuria made extensive use of spies, and Port Arthur, with all its defects of fortification and equipment, was known thoroughly inside and out to the Japanese general staff before they ever fired a shot at it.

In the field service regulations of the German army a paragraph directed that the service of protection in the field—that is to say, outposts, advanced guards, and reconnaissances—should always be assisted by a system of spying, and although this paragraph no longer stands in the book, the spirit of it is none the less carried out.

The field spies are a recognised and efficient arm.

Frederick the Great is recorded to have said: "When Marshal Subise goes to war, he is followed by a hundred cooks, but when I take the field I am preceded by a hundred spies."

The present leader of the German army might well say the same, though probably his "hundred" would amount to thousands.

We hear of them dressed in plain clothes as peasants, and signalling with coloured lights, with puffs of smoke from chimneys, and by using the church clock hands as semaphores.

Very frequently a priest was arrested and found to be a spy disguised, and as such he was shot. Also a German chauffeur in a French uniform, who had for some time been driving French staff officers about, was found to be a spy, and so met his death.

Early in the present war the German field spies had their secret code of signs, so that by drawing sketches of cattle of different colours and sizes on gates, etc., they conveyed information to each other of the strength and direction of different bodies of hostile troops in the neighbourhood.

As a rule, these are residential spies, who have lived for months or years as small tradesmen, etc., in the towns and villages now included in the theatre of war. On the arrival of the German invaders they have chalked on their doors, "Not to be destroyed. Good people here," and have done it for some of their neighbours also in order to divert suspicion. In their capacity of naturalised inhabitants they are in position, of course, to gain valuable tactical information for the commanders of the troops. And their different ways of communicating it are more than ingenious.

In some cases both spies and commanders have maps ruled off in small squares. The watchful spy signals to his commander, "Enemy's cavalry halted behind wood in square E15," and very soon a salvo of shells visits this spot. A woman spy was caught signalling with an electric flash lamp. Two different men (one of them an old one-legged stonebreaker at the roadside) were caught with field telephones hidden on them with wire coiled round their bodies. Shepherds with lanterns went about on the downs at night dodging the lanterns about in various ways which did not seem altogether necessary for finding sheep. Wireless telegraphs were set up to look like supports to iron chimneys.

In the South African Campaign a Dutch stationmaster acted as field spy for the Boers for a short time. It was only a very short time. His town and station were captured by my force, and, in order to divert suspicion, he cut and pulled down the telegraph wires, all except one, which was left in working order. By this wire he sent to the Boer headquarters all the information he could get about our forces and plans. Unfortunately, we had a party of men tapping the wire, and were able to read all his messages, and to confront him with them shortly afterwards.

Another stationmaster, in our own territory, acted as spy to the enemy before the war began by employing enemies as gangers and platelayers along the line with a view to the destruction of bridges and culverts as soon as war was declared. There was also found in his office a code by which the different arms of the service were designated in terms of timber for secretly telegraphing information. Thus:

Beams   meant Brigades

Timbers	"	Batteries
Logs	"	Guns
Scantlings	"	Battalions
Joists	"	Squadrons
Planks	"	Companies

THE PLUCK OF A SPY

Except in the case of the traitor spy, one does not quite understand why a spy should necessarily be treated worse than any other combatant, nor why his occupation should be looked upon as contemptible, for, whether in peace or war, his work is of a very exacting and dangerous kind. It is intensely exciting, and though in some cases it brings a big reward, the best spies are unpaid men who are doing it for the love of the thing, and as a really effective step to gaining something valuable for their country and for their side.

The plea put forward by the German spy, Lieut. Carl Lody, at his court-martial in London, was that "he would not cringe for mercy. He was not ashamed of anything that he had done; he was in honour bound not to give away the names of those who had employed him on this mission; he was not paid for it, he did it for his country's good, and he knew that he carried his life in his hands in doing so. Many a Briton was probably doing the same for Britain."

He was even spoken of in our House of Commons as being "a patriot who had died for his country as much as any soldier who fell in the field."

To be a really effective spy, a man has to be endowed with a strong spirit of self-sacrifice, courage, and self-control, with the power of acting a part, quick at observation and deduction, and blessed with good health and nerve of exceptional quality. A certain amount of scientific training is of value where a man has to be able to take the angles of a fort, or to establish the geological formation, say, of the middle island under the Forth Bridge, which was shown by Graves to be readily adaptable for explosion purposes.

For anyone who is tired of life, the thrilling life of a spy should be the very finest recuperator!

TRAITOROUS SPYING

Quite another class of spy is the traitor who gives away the secrets of his own country. For him, of course, there is no excuse. Fortunately, the Briton is not as a rule of a corruptible character, and many foreign spies in England have been discovered through their attempts to bribe officers or men to give away secrets.

On the other hand, we hear frequently of foreign soldiers falling victims to such temptation, and eventually being discovered. Cases have only recently come to light in Austria where officers were willing to sell information as regards a number of secret block-houses which were built on the frontier of Bukovina last year. Details of them got into the hands of another Power within a few days of the designs being made.

Apparently when suspicion falls upon an officer in Austria the case is not tried in public, but is conducted privately, sometimes by the Emperor himself. When the man is found guilty, the procedure is for four friends of the accused to visit him and tell him what has been discovered against him, and to present him with a loaded revolver and leave him. They then remain watching the house, in order that he shall not escape, and until he elects to shoot himself; if he fails to do so, in reasonable time, they go in and finish him off between them.

THE GERMAN SPY ORGANISATION

The espionage system of the Germans far exceeds that of any other country in its extent, cost, and organisation. It was thoroughly exposed after the war with France in 1870, when it was definitely shown that the German Government had an organisation of over 20,000 paid informers stationed in France, and controlled by one man, Stieber, for both political and military purposes.

To such completeness were their machinations carried that when Jules Favre came to Versailles to treat about the surrender of Paris with the headquarter staff of the German army he was met at the station by a carriage, of which the coachman was a German spy, and was taken to lodge in the house which was the actual headquarters of the spy department. Stieber himself was the valet, recommended to him as "a thoroughly trustworthy servant." Stieber availed himself of his position to go through his master's pockets and despatch cases daily, collecting most valuable data and information for Bismarck.

Somehow, on the surface, suspicion of the German spy methods seemed to have subsided since that date, although at the time widely known throughout Europe. But their methods have been steadily elaborated and carried into practice ever since, not in France alone, but in all the countries on the Continent, and also in Great Britain.

THE VALUE OF BEING STUPID

Fortunately for us, we are as a nation considered by the others to be abnormally stupid, therefore easily to be spied upon. But it is not always safe to judge entirely by appearances.

Our Ambassador at Constantinople some years ago had the appearance of a cheery, bluff, British farmer, with nothing below the surface in his character, and he was therefore looked upon as fair game by all his intriguing rivals in Eastern politics. It was only after repeated failures of their different missions they found that in every case they were out-intrigued by this innocent-looking gentleman, who below the surface was as cunning as a fox and as clever a diplomat as could be found in all the service.

And so it has been with us British. Foreign spies stationed in our country saw no difficulty in completely hoodwinking so stupid a people; they never supposed that the majority of them have all been known to our Secret Service Department, and carefully watched, unknown to themselves.

Few of them ever landed in this country without undergoing the scrutiny of an unobtrusive little old gentleman with tall hat and umbrella, but the wag of whose finger sent a detective on the heels of the visitor until his actual business and location were assured and found to be satisfactory.

For years the correspondence of these gentry has been regularly opened, noted, and sent on. They were not as a rule worth arresting, the information sent was not of any urgent importance, and so long as they went on thinking that they were unnoticed, their superiors in their own country made no effort to send more astute men in their place. Thus we knew what the enemy were looking for, and we knew what information they had received, and this as a rule was not of much account.

On August 4th, the day before the declaration of war, the twenty leading spies were formally arrested and over 200 of their minor agents were also taken in hand, and thus their organisation failed them at the moment when it was wanted most. Steps were also taken to prevent any substitutes being appointed in their places.

Private wireless stations were dismantled, and by means of traps those were discovered which had not been voluntarily reported and registered.

It used to amuse some of us to watch the foreign spies at work on our ground. One especially interested me, who set himself up ostensibly as a coal merchant, but never dealt in a single ounce of coal. His daily reconnaissance of the country, his noting of the roads, and his other movements entailed in preparing his reports, were all watched and recorded. His letters were opened in the post, sealed up, and sent on. His friends were observed and shadowed on arriving—as they did—at Hull instead of in London. And all the time he was plodding along, wasting his time, quite innocent of the fact that he was being watched, and was incidentally giving us a fine amount of information.

Another came only for a few hours, and was away again before we could collar him; but, knowing his moves, and what photographs he had taken, I was able to write to him, and tell him that had I known beforehand that he wished to photograph these places, I could have supplied him with some ready made, as the forts which they recorded were now obsolete.

On the other hand, the exceedingly stupid Englishmen who wandered about foreign countries sketching cathedrals, or catching butterflies, or fishing for trout, were merely laughed at as harmless lunatics. These have even invited officials to look at their sketch-books, which, had they had any suspicion or any eyes in their heads, would have revealed plans and armaments of their own fortresses interpolated among the veins of the botanist's drawings of leaves or on the butterflies' wings of the entomologist. Some examples of secret sketches of fortresses which have been used with success are shown on the following pages.

This sketch of a butterfly contains the outline of a fortress, and marks both the position and power of the guns. The marks on the wings <u>between</u> the lines mean nothing, but those <u>on</u> the lines show the nature and size of the guns, according to the keys below.

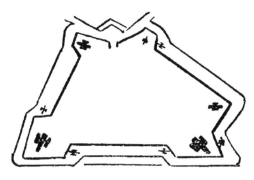

The marks on the wings reveal the shape of the fortress shown here and the size of the guns.

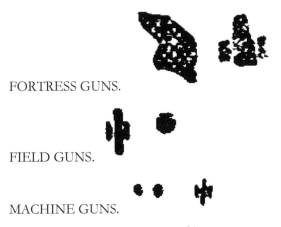

FORTRESS GUNS.

FIELD GUNS.

MACHINE GUNS.

The position of each gun is at the place inside the outline of the fort on the butterfly where the line marked with the spot ends. The head of the butterfly points towards the north.

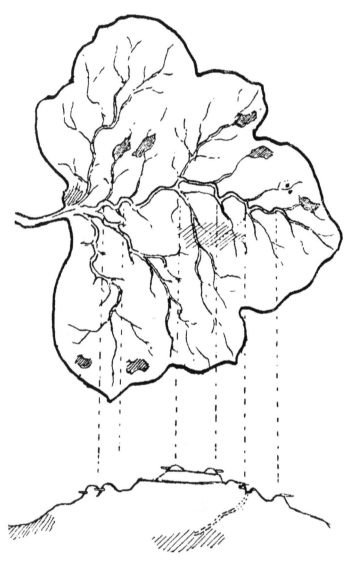

A smart piece of spy-work. Veins on an ivy leaf show the outline of the fort as seen looking west (Point of the leaf indicates north.)

Shows where big guns are mounted if a vein points to them.

Shows "dead ground," where there is shelter from fire.

Shows machine guns.

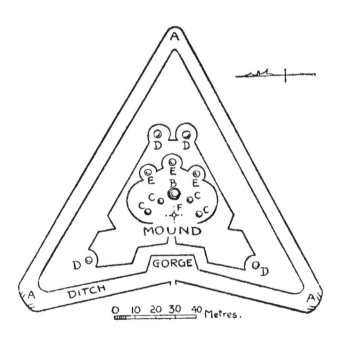

- 33 -

Here is another of the methods by which I concealed the plans of the forts I made.

First of all, I would sketch the plan as shown in the picture above giving the strength and positions of the various guns as shown below:

A. Kaponiers with machine guns.

B. 15 cm. gun cupola.

C. 12 cm. guns cupolas.

D. Q.-F. disappearing guns.

E. Howitzer cupolas.

F. Searchlight.

Having done this, I would consider the best method of concealing my plans. In this case I decided to transform the sketch into that of a stained glass window, and if you will carefully examine the picture above you will see how successfully this has been done. Certain of the decorations signify the sizes and positions of the guns. These signs are given below, together with their meaning.

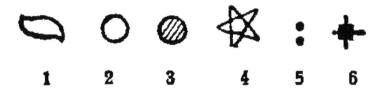

1. 15 *cm. gun.*

2. *Howitzers.*

3. *Q.-F. disappearing guns.*

4. 12 *cm. guns.*

5. *Machine guns.*

6. *Searchlight.*

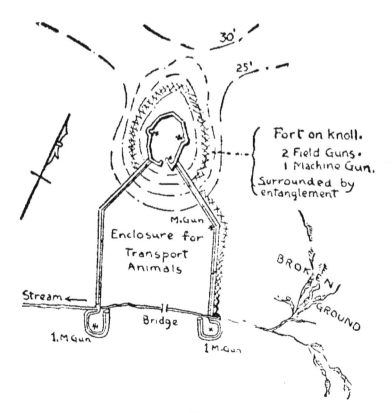

Fort on knoll.
2 Field Guns.
1 Machine Gun.
Surrounded by entanglement

CONCEALING A FORT IN A MOTH'S HEAD

Another example of this method of making secret plans is shown here.

This sketch was made, giving all the particulars that I wanted. I then decided to bury it in such a way that it could not be recognised as a fortress plan if I were caught by the military authorities. One idea which occurred to me was to make it into the doorway of a cathedral or church, but I finally decided on the sketch of the moth's head. Underneath in my note-book I wrote the following words:—

> *"Head of Dula moth as seen through a magnifying glass. Caught 19.5.12. Magnified about six times size of life."*
> *(Meaning scale of 6 inches to the mile.)*

BUTTERFLY HUNTING IN DALMATIA

Once I went "butterfly hunting" in Dalmatia. Cattaro, the capital, has been the scene of much bombarding during the present war.

More than a hundred years ago it was bombarded by the British fleet and taken. It was then supposed to be impregnable. It lies at the head of a loch some fifteen miles long, and in some parts but a few hundred yards wide, in a trough between mountains. From Cattaro, at the head of the loch, a zig-zag road leads up the mountain side over the frontier into Montenegro.

When the British ships endeavoured to attack from the seaward, the channel was closed by chains and booms put across it. But the defenders had reckoned without the resourcefulness of the British "handyman," and a few days later, to the utter astonishment of the garrison, guns began to bombard them from the top of a neighbouring mountain!

The British captain had landed his guns on the Adriatic shore, and by means of timber slides rigged up on the mountain side he had hauled his guns bodily up the rocky steeps to the very summit of the mountain.

He fixed up his batteries, and was eventually able to bombard the town with such effect that it had to surrender.

It was perhaps characteristic of us that we only took the town because it was held by our enemies. We did not want it, and when we had got it we did not know what to do with it. We therefore handed it over to the Montenegrins, and thus gave them a seaport of their own. For this feat the Montenegrins have always had a feeling of admiration and of gratitude to the British, and, though by terms of ulterior treaties it was eventually handed over to Dalmatia, the Montenegrins have never forgotten our goodwill towards them on this occasion.

But other batteries have since been built upon these mountain tops, and it was my business to investigate their positions, strength, and armaments.

I went armed with most effective weapons for the purpose, which have served me well in many a similar campaign. I took a sketch-book, in which were numerous pictures—some finished, others only partly done—of butterflies of every degree and rank, from a "Red Admiral" to a "Painted Lady."

Carrying this book and a colour-box, and a butterfly net in my hand, I was above all suspicion to anyone who met me on the lonely mountain side, even in the neighbourhood of the forts.

I was hunting butterflies, and it was always a good introduction with which to go to anyone who was watching me with suspicion. Quite frankly, with my sketch-book in hand, I would ask innocently whether he had seen such-and-such a butterfly in the neighbourhood, as I was anxious to catch one. Ninety-nine out of a hundred did not know one butterfly from another—any more than I do—so one was on fairly safe ground in that way, and they thoroughly sympathised with the mad Englishman who was hunting these insects.

They did not look sufficiently closely into the sketches of butterflies to notice that the delicately drawn veins of the wings were exact representations, in plan, of their own fort, and that the spots on the wings denoted the number and position of guns and their different calibres.

On another occasion I found it a simple disguise to go as a fisherman into the country which I wanted to examine.

My business was to find some passes in the mountains, and report whether they were feasible for the passage of troops. I therefore wandered up the various streams which led over the hills, and by quietly fishing about I was able to make surveys of the whole neighbourhood.

But on one occasion a countryman constituted himself my guide, and insisted on sticking to me all the morning, showing me places where fish could be caught. I was not, as a matter of fact, much of a fisherman at that time, nor had I any desire to catch fish, and my tackle was of a very ramshackle description for the purpose.

I flogged the water assiduously with an impossible fly, just to keep the man's attention from my real work, in the hope that he would eventually get tired of it and go away. But not he! He watched me with the greatest interest for a long time, and eventually explained that he did not know anything about fly fishing, but had a much better system of getting the fish together before casting a worm or slug-among-them.

His system he then proceeded to demonstrate, which was to spit into the water. This certainly attracted a run of fish, and then he said that if only he had a worm he could catch any number.

I eventually got rid of him by sending him to procure such, and while he was away I made myself scarce and clambered over the ridge to another valley.

HOW SPIES DISGUISE THEMSELVES

Spying brings with it a constant wearing strain of nerves and mind, seeing that it involves certain death for a false step in war or imprisonment in peace. The Government promises to give no help whatever to its servant if caught. He is warned to keep no notes, to confide in no one, to use disguises where necessary, and to shift for himself entirely.

The matter of disguise is not so much one of theatrical make-up as of being able to secure a totally different character in voice and mannerisms, and especially of gait in walking and appearance from behind. A man may effect a wonderful disguise in front, yet be instantly recognised by a keen eye from behind. This is a point which is frequently forgotten by beginners, and yet is one of the most important. The first and third figures show an effective make-up in front, but the second figure, a back-view, shows how easily the man may be recognised by a person behind him. The fourth and fifth sketches show, by means of dotted lines, how the "back-view" can be altered by change of clothing and gait.

The matter of disguise is not so much one of a theatrical make-up—although this is undoubtedly a useful art—as of being able to assume a totally different character, change of voice and mannerisms, especially of gait in walking and appearance from behind.

This point is so often forgotten by beginners, and yet it is one of the most important.

I was at one time watched by a detective who one day was a soldierly-looking fellow and the next an invalid with a patch over his eye. I could not believe it was the same man until I watched him from behind and saw him walking, when at once his individuality was apparent.

For mannerisms, a spy has by practice to be able to show an impediment in his speech one day, whereas the next a wiggle of an eyelid or a snuffling at the nose will make him appear a totally different being.

For a quick change, it is wonderful what difference is made by merely altering your hat and necktie. It is usual for a person addressing another to take note of his necktie, and probably of his hat, if of nothing else, and thus it is often useful to carry a necktie and a cap of totally different hue from that which you are wearing, ready to change immediately in order to escape recognition a few minutes later.

This illustration shows how the writer was able to disguise himself at very short notice when he observed that he was recognised on a railway station. The first sketch shows him as he entered a waiting-room shortly after his suspicions were aroused. The second depicts him on his exit a few minutes later. The disguise, simple though it may seem, was entirely successful.

I learnt this incidentally through being interviewed some years ago at a railway station. A few minutes after the ordeal I found myself close up to my interviewer, when he was re-telling the incident to a brother journalist, who was also eager to find me. "He is down there, in one of the last carriages of the train. You will know him at once; he is wearing a green Homburg hat and a red tie, and a black coat."

Fortunately I had a grey overcoat on my arm, in which was a travelling cap and a comforter. Diving into the waiting-room, I effected a "quick change" into these, crammed my hat into my pocket, and tottered back, with an invalid shuffle, to my carriage. I re-entered it under the nose of the waiting reporter without being suspected, and presently had the pleasure of being carried away before him unassailed.

On a recent occasion in my knowledge a man was hunted down into a back street which was a *cul-de-sac*, with no exit from it. He turned into the door of a warehouse and went up some flights of stairs, hoping to find a refuge, but, finding none, he turned back and came down again and faced the crowd which was waiting outside, uncertain which house he had entered.

By assuming extreme lameness in one leg, hunching up one shoulder, and jamming his hat down over a distorted-looking face, he was able to limp boldly down among them without one of them suspecting his individuality.

In regard to disguises, hair on the face—such as moustache or beard—are very usually resorted to for altering a man's appearance but these are perfectly useless in the eye of a trained detective unless the eyebrows also are changed in some way.

Another instance of how an effective disguise can be assumed on the spur of the moment. This disguise was effected in two minutes.

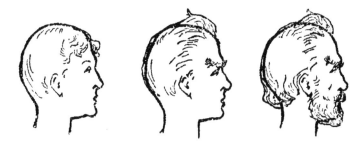

The use of hair in disguising the face is perfectly useless unless the eyebrows are considerably changed. The brow and the back of the head are also extremely important factors in the art of disguise.

The second picture shows the effect of "improving" the eyebrows of the face on the left, and also of raising the hair on the brow, while the third sketch shows what a difference the addition of a beard and extra hair on the back of the head, can make.

I remember meeting a man on the veldt in South Africa bronzed and bearded, who came to me and said that he had been at school with one of my name. As he thrust his hat back on his head I at once recognised the brow which I had last seen at Charterhouse some twenty-five years before, and the name and nickname at once sprang to my lips. "Why, you are Liar Jones," I exclaimed. He said, "My name is Jones, but I was not aware of the 'Liar.'"

"In altering your face you must remember that 'improved' eyebrows alter the expression of the face more than any beards, shaving, etc. Tattoo marks can be painted on the hands or arms, to be washed off when you change your disguise.... Disguising by beginners is almost invariably overdone in front and not enough behind.... Before attempting to be a spy first set yourself to catch a spy, and thus learn what faults to avoid as likely to give you away." [*Aids to Scouting*, p. 136.]

It fell to my lot at one time to live as a plumber in South-east London, and I grew a small "goatee" beard, which was rather in vogue amongst men of that class at that time.

One day, in walking past the Naval and Military Club in Piccadilly in my workman's get-up, I passed an old friend, a major in the Horse Artillery, and almost without thinking I accosted him by his regimental nickname. He stared and wondered, and then supposed that I had been a man in his battery, and could not believe his eyes when I revealed my identity.

I was never suspected by those among whom I went, and with whom I became intimate. I had nominally injured my arm in an accident and carried it in a sling, and was thus unable to work, or what was also a blessing, to join in fights in which my friends from time to time got involved. My special companion was one Jim Bates, a carpenter. I lost sight of him for some years, and when next I met him he was one of the crowd at a review at Aldershot, where I was in full rig as an Hussar officer. It was difficult to persuade him that I was his former friend the plumber.

Later on, when employed on a reconnaissance mission in South Africa, I had grown a red beard to an extent that would have disguised me from my own mother. Coming out of the post office of a small country town, to my surprise I came up against the Colonel of my regiment, who was there for an outing. I at once—forgetting my disguise—accosted him with a cheery "Hullo, Colonel, I didn't know you were here," and he turned on me and stared for a minute or two, and then responded huffily that he did not know who I was. As he did not appear to want to, I went my ways, and only reminded him months later of our brief meeting!

THE SPORT OF SPYING

Undoubtedly spying would be an intensely interesting sport even if no great results were obtainable from it. There is a fascination which gets hold of anyone who has tried the art. Each day brings fresh situations and conditions requiring quick change of action and originality to meet them.

Here are a few instances from actual experiences. None of these are anything out of the common, but are merely the everyday doings of the average agent, but they may best explain the sporting value of the work.

One of the attractive features of the life of a spy is that he has, on occasion, to be a veritable Sherlock Holmes. He has to notice the smallest of details, points which would probably escape the untrained eye, and then he has to put this and that together and deduce a meaning from them.

I remember once when carrying out a secret reconnaissance in South Africa I came across a farmhouse from which the owner was absent at the moment of my arrival. I had come far and would have still further to go before I came across any habitation, and I was hard up for a lodging for the night.

After off-saddling and knee-haltering my horse, I looked into the various rooms to see what sort of a man was the inhabitant. It needed only a glance into his bedroom in this ramshackle hut to see that he was one of the right sort, for there, in a glass on the window-sill, were two tooth-brushes.

I argued that he was an Englishman and of cleanly habits, and would do for me as a host—and I was not mistaken in the result!

THE VALUE OF HIDE-AND-SEEK

The game of Hide-and-Seek is really one of the best games for a boy, and can be elaborated until it becomes scouting in the field. It teaches you a lot.

I was strongly addicted to it as a child, and the craft learned in that innocent field of sport has stood me in good stead in many a critical time since. To lie flat in a furrow among the currant bushes when I had not time to reach the neighbouring box bushes before the pursuer came in sight taught me the value of not using the most obvious cover, since it would at once be searched. The hunters went at once to the box bushes as the likely spot, while I could watch their doings from among the stems of the currant bushes.

Often I have seen hostile scouts searching the obvious bits of cover, but they did not find *me* there; and, like the elephant hunter among the fern trees, or a boar in a cotton crop, so a boy in the currant bushes is invisible to the enemy, while he can watch every move of the enemy's legs.

This I found of value when I came to be pursued by mounted military police, who suspected me of being a spy at some manoeuvres abroad. After a rare chase I scrambled over a wall and dropped into an orchard of low fruit trees. Here squatting in a ditch, I watched the legs of the gendarmes' horses while they quartered the plantation, and when they drew away from me I crept to the bank of a deep water channel which formed one of the boundaries of the enclosure. Here I found a small plank bridge by which I could cross, but before doing so I loosened the near end, and passed over, dragging the plank after me.

On the far side the country was open, and before I had gone far the gendarmes spied me, and after a hurried consultation, dashed off at a gallop for the nearest bridge, half a mile away. I promptly turned back, replaced my bridge and recrossed the stream, throwing the plank into the river, and made my way past the village to the next station down the line while the horsemen were still hunting for me in the wrong place.

Another secret that one picked up at the game of Hide-and-Seek was, if possible, to get above the level of the hunter's eye, and to "freeze"—that is, to sit tight without a movement, and, although not in actual concealment, you are very apt to escape notice by so doing. I found it out long ago by lying flat along the top of an ivy-clad wall when my pursuers passed within a few feet of me without looking up at me. I put it to the proof later on by sitting on a bank beside the road, just above the height of a man, but so near that I might have touched a passer-by with a fishing-rod; and there I sat without any concealment and counted fifty-four wayfarers, out of whom no more than eleven noticed me.

The knowledge of this fact came in useful on one of my investigating tours. Inside a great high wall lay a dockyard in which, it was rumoured, a new power-house was being erected, and possibly a dry dock was in course of preparation.

It was early morning; the gates were just opened; the workmen were beginning to arrive, and several carts of materials were waiting to come in. Seizing the opportunity of the gates being open, I gave a hurried glance in, as any ordinary passer-by might do. I was promptly ejected by the policeman on duty in the lodge.

I did not go far. My intention was to get inside somehow and to see what I could. I watched the first of the carts go in, and noticed that the policeman was busily engaged in talking to the leading wagoner, while the second began to pass through the gate. In a moment I jumped alongside it on the side opposite to the janitor, and so passed in and continued to walk with the vehicle as it turned to the right and wound its way round the new building in course of construction.

I then noticed another policeman ahead of me and so I kept my position by the cart, readapting its cover in order to avoid him. Unfortunately in rounding the corner I was spied by the first policeman, and he immediately began to shout to me (*see map*). I was deaf to his remarks and walked on as unconcernedly as a guilty being could till I placed the corner of the new building between him and me. Then I fairly hooked it along the back of the building and rounded the far corner of it. As I did so I saw out of the tail of my eye that he was coming full speed after me and was calling policeman No. 2 to his aid. I darted like a red-shank round the next corner out of sight of both policemen, and looked for a method of escape.

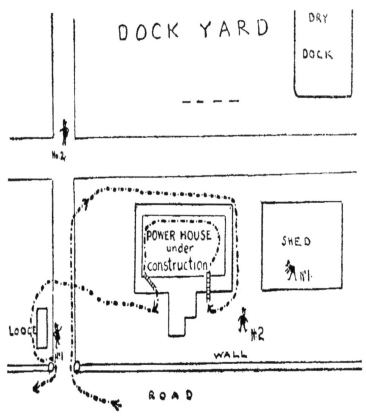

The dotted line in this plan shows my route, small figures are policemen looking for me.

The scaffolding of the new house towered above me, and a ladder led upwards on to it. Up this I went like a lamplighter, keeping one eye on the corner of the building lest I should be followed.

I was half-way up when round the corner came one of the policemen. I at once "froze." I was about fifteen feet above sea level and not twenty yards from him. He stood undecided with his legs well apart, peering from side to side in every direction to see where I had gone, very anxious and shifty. I was equally anxious but immovable.

Presently he drew nearer to the ladder and, strangely enough, I felt safer when he came below me, and he passed almost under me, looking in at the doorways of the unfinished building. Then he doubtfully turned and looked back at a shed behind him, thinking I might have gone in there, and finally started off, and ran on round the next corner of the building. The moment he disappeared I finished the rest of my run up the ladder and safely reached the platform of the scaffolding.

The workmen were not yet upon the building, so I had the whole place to myself. My first act was to look for another ladder as a line of escape in case of being chased. It is always well to have a back door to your hiding place; that is one of the essentials in scouting.

Presently I found a short ladder leading from my platform to the stage below, but it did not go to the ground. Peering quietly over the scaffolding, I saw my friend the policeman below, still at fault. I blessed my stars that he was no tracker, and therefore had not seen my footmarks leading to the foot of the ladder.

Then I proceeded to take note of my surroundings and to gather information. Judging from the design of the building, its great chimneys, etc., I was actually on the new power-house. From my post I had an excellent view over the dockyard, and within 100 feet of me were the excavation works of the new dock, whose dimensions I could easily estimate.

I whipped out my prismatic compass and quickly took the bearings of two conspicuous points on the neighbouring hills, and so fixed the position which could be marked on a large scale map for purposes of shelling the place, if desired.

Meantime my pursuer had called the other policeman to him, and they were in close confabulation immediately below me, where I could watch them through a crack between two of the foot-boards. They had evidently come to the conclusion that I was not in the power-house as the interior was fully open to view, and they had had a good look into it. Their next step was to examine the goods shed close by, which was evidently full of building lumber, etc.

One man went into it while the other remained outside on the line that I should probably take for escaping, that is, between it and the boundary wall leading to the gateway. By accident rather than by design he stood close to the foot of my ladder, and thus cut off my retreat in that direction. While they were thus busy they were leaving the gate unguarded, and I thought it was too good a chance to be missed, so, returning along the scaffolding until I reached the small ladder, I climbed down this on to the lower story, and, seeing no one about, I quickly swarmed down one of the scaffolding poles and landed safely on the ground close behind the big chimney of the building.

Here I was out of sight, although not far from the policeman guarding the ladder; and, taking care to keep the corner of the building between us, I made my way round to the back of the lodge, and then slipped out of the gate without being seen.

SPYING ON MOUNTAIN TROOPS

I was once in a country where the mountain troops on their frontier were said to be of a wonderfully efficient kind, but nobody knew much about their organisation or equipment or their methods of working, so I was sent to see if I could find out anything about them, I got in amongst the mountains at the time when their annual manoeuvres were going on, and I found numbers of troops quartered in the valleys and billeted in all the villages. But these all appeared to be the ordinary type of troops, infantry, artillery of the line, etc. The artillery were provided with sledges by which the men could pull the guns up the mountain sides with ropes, and the infantry were supplied with alpenstocks to help them in getting over the bad ground. For some days I watched the manoeuvres, but saw nothing very striking to report.

Then one evening in passing through a village where they were billeted I saw a new kind of soldier coming along with three pack mules. He evidently belonged to those mountain forces of which, so far, I had seen nothing. I got into conversation with him, and found that he had come down from the higher ranges in order to get supplies for his company which was high up among the snow peaks, and entirely out of reach of the troops manoeuvring on the lower slopes.

He incidentally told me that the force to which he belonged was a very large one, composed of artillery and infantry, and that they were searching amongst the glaciers and the snows for another force which was coming as an enemy against them, and they hoped to come into contact with them probably the very next day. He then roughly indicated to me the position in which his own force was bivouacking that night, on the side of a high peak called the "Wolf's Tooth."

By condoling with him on the difficult job he would have to get through, and suggesting impossible roads by which he could climb, he eventually let out to me exactly the line which the path took, and I recognised that it would be possible to arrive there during the night without being seen.

So after dark, when the innkeeper thought I was safely in bed, I quietly made my way up the mountain side to where the "Wolf's Tooth" stood up against the starry sky as a splendid landmark to guide me. There was no difficulty in passing through the village with its groups of soldiers strolling about off duty, but on the roads leading out of it many sentries were posted, and I feared that they would scarcely let me pass without inquiring as to who I was and where I was going.

So I spent a considerable time in trying to evade these, and was at last fortunate in discovering a storm drain leading between high walls up a steep bank into an orchard, through which I was able to slip away unseen by the sentries guarding the front of the village. I climbed up by such paths and goat tracks as I could find leading in the direction desired. I failed to strike the mule path indicated by my friend the driver, but with the peak of the Wolf's Tooth outlined above me against the stars, I felt that I could not go far wrong—and so it proved in the event.

It was a long and arduous climb, but just as dawn began to light up the eastern sky I found myself safely on the crest, and the twinkling of the numerous camp fires showed me where the force was bivouacked which I had come to see.

As the daylight came on the troops began to get on the move, and, after early coffee, were beginning to spread themselves about the mountain side, taking up positions ready for attack or defence, so as it grew lighter I hastened to find for myself a comfortable little knoll, from which I hoped to be able to see all that went on without myself being seen; and for a time all went particularly well.

Troops deployed themselves in every direction. Look-out men with telescopes were posted to spy on the neighbouring hills, and I could see where the headquarters staff were gathered together to discuss the situation. Gradually they came nearer to the position I myself was occupying, and divided themselves into two parties; the one with the general remained standing where they were, while the other came in the direction of the mound on which I was lying.

Then to my horror some of them began to ascend my stronghold.

I at once stood up and made no further efforts at concealment, but got out my sketch book and started to make a drawing of "Dawn Among the Mountains." I was very soon noticed, and one or two officers walked over to me and entered into conversation, evidently anxious to find out who I was and what was my business there.

My motto is that a smile and a stick will carry you through any difficulty; the stick was obviously not politic on this occasion; I therefore put on a double extra smile and showed them my sketch book, explaining that the one ambition of my life was to make a drawing of the Wolf's Tooth by sunrise.

They expressed a respectful interest, and then explained that their object in being there was to make an attack from the Wolf's Tooth on the neighbouring mountain, provided that the enemy were actually in possession of it. I on my part showed a mild but tactful interest in their proceedings.

The less interest I showed, the more keen they seemed to be to explain matters to me, until eventually I had the whole of their scheme exposed before me, illustrated by their own sketch maps of the district, which were far more detailed and complete than anything of the kind I had seen before.

In a short time we were on the best of terms; they had coffee going which they shared with me, while I distributed my cigarettes and chocolates amongst them. They expressed surprise at my having climbed up there at that early hour, but were quite satisfied when I explained that I came from Wales, and at once jumped to the conclusion that I was a Highlander, and asked whether I wore a kilt when I was at home.

In the middle of our exchange of civilities the alarm was given that the enemy was in sight, and presently we saw through our glasses long strings of men coming from all directions towards us over the snows. Between us and the enemy lay a vast and deep ravine with almost perpendicular sides, traversed here and there by zig-zagging goat tracks.

Officers were called together, the tactics of the fight were described to them, and in a few minutes the battalion and company commanders were scattered about studying with their glasses the opposite mountain, each, as they explained to me at the time, picking out for himself and for his men a line for ascending to the attack.

Then the word was given for the advance, and the infantry went off in long strings of men armed with alpenstocks and ropes. Ropes were used for lowering each other down bad places, and for stringing the men together when they got on to the snows to save them from falling into crevasses, etc. But the exciting point of the day was when the artillery proceeded to move down into the ravine; the guns were all carried in sections on the backs of mules, as well as their ammunition and spare parts.

In a few minutes tripods were erected, the mules were put into slings, guns and animals were then lowered one by one into the depths below until landed on practicable ground. Here they were loaded up again and got into their strings for climbing up the opposite mountains, and in an incredibly short space of time both mules and infantry were to be seen, like little lines of ants, climbing by all the available tracks which could be found leading towards the ice fields above.

The actual results of the field day no longer interested me; I had seen what I had come for—the special troops, their guns, their supply and hospital arrangements, their methods of moving in this apparently impassable country, and their maps and ways of signalling.

All was novel, all was practical. For example, on looking at one of the maps shown to me, I remarked that I should have rather expected to find on it every goat track marked, but the officer replied that there was no need for that; every one of his men was born in this valley, and knew every goat track over the mountain. Also a goat track did not remain for more than a few weeks, or at most a few months, owing to landslips and washouts; they are continually being altered, and to mark them on a map would lead to confusion.

POSING AS AN ARTIST

My mountain climbing came into use on another occasion of a somewhat similar kind. A map had been sent me by my superiors of a mountainous district in which it had been stated that three forts had recently been built. It was only known generally what was the situation of these forts, and no details had been secured as to their size or armament.

On arriving at the only town in the neighbourhood, my first few days were spent strolling about looking generally at the mountains amongst which the forts were supposed to be. I had meantime made the acquaintance through my innkeeper of one or two local sportsmen of the place, and I inquired among them as to the possibilities of partridge or other shooting among the mountains when the season came on.

I told them that I enjoyed camping out for a few days at a time in such country for sketching and shooting purposes. I asked as to the possibilities of hiring tents and mules to carry them, and a good muleteer was recommended to me, who knew the whole of the countryside, and could tell me all the likely spots that there were for camping grounds.

Eventually I engaged him to take me for a day or two in exploring the neighbourhood, with a view to fixing on camping grounds and seeing the view. We went for a considerable distance along a splendid high road which led up into the mountains. As we got into the high parts he suggested that we should leave the road and clamber down into the ravine, along which we could go for some distance and then reascend and rejoin the road higher up.

He then explained that this was a military road, and that it would be desirable to leave it for a space in order to avoid the guard-house upon it, where a sentry was posted with orders to allow no one beyond that point.

We successfully evaded the guard-house according to his direction, and eventually found ourselves on the road again, in a position well up towards the top of the ridge; but on our left as we progressed up the road was a steep minor ridge which we presently proceeded to ascend.

When we were near the top he said to me with a knowing grin:—

"Now if you look over there, you will see before you exactly what you want."

And as I looked over I found below me one of the new forts. It was exactly what I wanted to see spread before my eyes like a map. I simply had to take a bird's-eye view of it to get its complete plan.

Beyond it on another ridge lay another fort, and almost behind me I could see part of the third, while beyond and above were still more forts up on the heights. I had got into a regular nest of them. My position on the ridge gave me a splendid view of mountains, and referring to them I said:—

"Yes, indeed, you have brought me to exactly the right spot."

But he grinned again maliciously, pointing down to the fort, and said:—

"Yes, but that is the best view of all, I think."

He seemed to grasp my intentions most fully. Far below the forts lay the straits which they were designed to protect for the vessels steaming through them. I started at once to make a sketch of the panorama, carefully omitting that ground where the forts lay, partly in order to disarm my friend's suspicions, and partly to protect me in the event of my arrest.

Presently my companion volunteered to go down to the fort and bring up his brother, who, he said, was a gunner stationed there, and could give me every detail that I could wish about their guns, etc.

This sounded almost too good to be true, but with the greatest indifference I said I should be glad to see him, and off went my friend. The moment that he was out of sight I took care to move off into a neighbouring kopje where I could hide myself in case of his bringing up a force of men to capture me.

From here I was able to make a pretty accurate sketch of the fort and its gun emplacements on the inside of the lining of my hat, and when I had replaced this I went on as hurriedly as possible with my sketch to show that I had been fully occupied during the guide's absence.

Presently I saw him returning, but as he was only accompanied by one other man, I crept down again to my original position and received them smiling.

The gunner was most communicative, and told me all about his guns and their sizes and what were their powers as regards range and accuracy. He told me that once a year an old vessel that was about to be broken up was towed along behind a steamer down the straits to afford a target to the defence forts as she passed on. He said regretfully:—

"We are number three fort, and so far, no vessel has ever successfully passed one and two—they always get sunk before they reach us"—and he gave me the exact range and the number of rounds fired, which showed that their shooting was pretty good.

Many other details I found out as to the number of the men, their feeding and hospital arrangements; and a few days later I was able to take myself home with a good stock of valuable information and the good wishes and hopes of my various friends that I some day would return to shoot the partridges. But I am certain that one man was not taken in by my professions, either as an artist or as a sportsman, and that was the muleteer.

FOOLING A GERMAN SENTRY

On another occasion I wanted to ascertain what value there was in the musketry training of a foreign infantry. Also it had been reported that they had recently acquired a new form of machine gun which was a particularly rapid firer and very accurate in its effects. Its calibre was known, and its general pattern (from photographs), but its actual capabilities were still a matter of conjecture.

On this occasion I thought the simplest way would be to go undisguised. Without any concealment I went to stay in garrison towns where I happened to know one or two officers. I obtained introductions to other officers, and gradually became their companion at meals and at their evening entertainments. They mounted me on their horses, I rode with them on their rounds of duty, and I came to be an attendant at their field days and manoeuvres; but whenever we approached the rifle ranges I was always politely but firmly requested to go no further, but to await their return, since the practice was absolutely confidential. I could gain no information from them as to what went on within the enclosure where the rifle range was hidden.

Two of my English friends one day incautiously stopped at the entrance gate to one of the ranges, and were promptly arrested and kept in the guard-room for some hours, and finally requested to leave the place, without getting much satisfaction out of it. So I saw that caution was necessary. Little by little, especially after some very cheerful evenings, I elicited a certain amount of information from my friends as to what the new machine gun did and was likely to do, and how their soldiers could of course never hit a running target, since it was with the greatest difficulty they hit the standing one at all. But more than this it was impossible to get.

However, I moved on to another military station, where as a stranger I tried another tack. The rifle ranges were surrounded by a belt of trees, outside of which was an unclimbable fence guarded by two sentries, one on either side. It seemed impossible to get into or even near the range without considerable difficulty.

One day I sauntered carelessly down in the direction of the range at a point far away from the entrance gate, and here I lay down on the grass as if to sleep, but in reality to listen and take the rate of the shooting from the sound and also the amount of success by the sound of the hits on the iron target. Having gained a certain amount of data in this way, I approached more nearly in the hope of getting a sight of what was going on.

While the sentry's back was turned I made a rush for the fence, and though I could not get over, I found a loose plank through which I was able to get a good view of what was happening.

While engaged at this, to my horror the sentry suddenly turned on his tracks and came back towards me. But I had been prepared against such eventualities, and jamming back the plank into its place, I produced from my pocket a bottle of brandy which I had brought for the purpose. Half of it had been already sprinkled over my clothes, so that when the man approached he found me in a state of drunkenness, smelling vilely of spirits, and profuse in my offers to him to share the bottle.

The above sketch shows the writer in a tight place. He was discovered in close proximity to a rifle range by a German sentry. He pretended to be intoxicated, and so escaped. But it was a close shave.

He could make nothing of me, and therefore gently but firmly conducted me to the end of his beat and thrust me forth and advised me to go home, which I did in great content....

A SPY IS SUSPICIOUS

The practice of spying has one unfortunate tendency: it teaches one to trust no one, not even a would-be benefactor. A foreign country had recently manufactured a new form of field gun which was undergoing extensive secret trials, which were being conducted in one of her colonies in order to avoid being watched. I was sent to find out particulars of this gun. On arrival in the colony I found that a battery of new guns was carrying out experiments at a distant point along the railway.

The place was by all description merely a roadside station, with not even a village near it, so it would be difficult to go and stay there without being noticed at once. The timetable, however, showed that the ordinary day train stopped there for half an hour for change of engines, so I resolved to see what I could do in the space of time allowed.

We jogged along in the local train happily enough and stopped at every little station as we went. At one of these a Colonial farmer entered my carriage, and though apparently ill and doleful, we got into conversation on the subject of the country and the crops.

At length we drew up at the station where the guns were said to be. Eagerly looking from the window, my delight may be imagined when I saw immediately outside the station yard the whole battery of guns standing parked.

Everybody left the train to stretch their legs, and I did not lose a moment in hurrying through the station and walking out to have a closer look at what I had come to see.

The sentry on the guns was on the further side from me, and therefore I was able to have a pretty close look at the breech action and various other items before he could come round to my side. But he very quickly noticed my presence, and not only came himself, but shouted to another man whom I had not so far seen behind a corner of the station wall.

This was the corporal of the guard, who rushed at me and began abusing me with every name he could lay his tongue to for being here without permit. I tried to explain that I was merely a harmless passenger by the train coming out to stretch my legs, and had never noticed his rotten old guns? But he quickly shoo'd me back into the station.

I betook myself once more to the carriage, got out my field glasses, and continued my investigations from the inside of the carriage, where I had quite a good view of the guns outside the station, and was able to note a good deal of information painted on them as to their weight, calibre, etc. Suddenly in the midst of my observations I found the view was obscured, and looking up, I found the face of the corporal peering in at me; he had caught me in the act. But nothing more came of it at the moment.

My farmer friend presently returned to his place, the whistle sounded, and the train lumbered on.

When I resumed conversation with the Colonist I remarked on his invalid appearance and enquired about his health. The poor man, with tears running down his cheeks, then confessed to me it was not illness of body, but worry of the mind that was preying upon him.

He had utterly failed in his attempt at making a successful farm, and had entered the train with the idea of cutting his throat, and would have done so had I not been there to prevent him. Life was over for him, and he did not know what to do. I got him to talk about his losses, and offered suggestions to him based on the experiences of a friend of mine who was also a farmer in that country, and who for ten years had failed until the right method came to him in the eleventh year, and he was now making his business a huge success.

This put hope at once into my volatile companion. He bucked up and became cheerful and confidential. Finally he said:

"You have done me a good turn. I will do something for you. I know that you are a German spy, and I know that you are going to be arrested at the station where this train stops for the night. You were spotted by a non-commissioned officer at the last station, and while I was in the telegraph office he came in and sent a telegram to the Commandant of the terminal station, reporting that a German spy had been examining the guns and was travelling by this train in this carriage."

I at once laughed genially at the mistake made, and explained to him that I was not a German at all. He replied that that would not avail me—I should be arrested all the same if I went on to the end of the journey.

"But," he suggested, "I shall be getting out myself at the very next station to go back to my farm, and my advice to you is to get out there also. You will find a good inn where you can put up for the night, and to-morrow morning the early train will take you on clean through that very station where the military commandant will be on the look-out for you to-night."

I replied that, as an Englishman, I had nothing to fear, and I should go on.

At the next station accordingly he got out, and after an affectionate farewell, I went on. But there was yet another station between this and the night stop, and on arrival there I took the hint of my friend and got out and spent the night at the little inn of the place. Following his advice still further, I took the early train next morning and ran through the place where they had been looking out for me. I had not got out when he invited me to at his station lest his invitation might merely have been a trap to test whether I was a spy; had I accepted it, no doubt he might have had friends at hand to arrange my arrest. As it was, I came away scot free with all the information I wanted about the new gun.

HOODWINKING A TURKISH SENTRY

A big new Turkish fort had been recently built, and my business was to get some idea of its plan and construction. From my inn in the town I sauntered out early one morning before sunrise, hoping to find no sentries awake, so that I could take the necessary angles and pace the desired bases in order to plot in a fairly accurate plan of it.

To some extent I had succeeded when I noticed among the sandhills another fellow looking about, and, it seemed to me, trying to dodge me. This was rather ominous, and I spent some of my time trying to evade this "dodger," imagining that he was necessarily one of the guard attempting my capture.

In evading him, unfortunately, I exposed myself rather more than usual to view from the fort, and presently was challenged by one of the sentries. I did not understand his language, but I could understand his gesture well enough when he presented his rifle and took deliberate aim at me. This induced me to take cover as quickly as might be behind a sandhill, where I sat down and waited for a considerable time to allow the excitement to cool down.

Presently, who should I see creeping round the corner of a neighbouring sandhill but my friend the "dodger"! It was too late to avoid him, and the moment he saw me he appeared to wish to go away rather than to arrest me. We then recognised that we were mutually afraid of each other, and therefore came together with a certain amount of diffidence on both sides.

However, we got into conversation, in French, and I very soon found that, although representatives of different nationalities, we were both at the same game of making a plan of the fort. We therefore joined forces, and behind a sandhill we compared notes as to what information we had already gained, and then devised a little plan by which to complete the whole scheme.

My friend took his place in a prominent position with his back to the fort and commenced to smoke, with every appearance of indifference to the defence work behind him. This was meant to catch the sentry's eye and attract his attention while I did some creeping and crawling and got round the other side of the work, where I was able to complete our survey in all its details.

A sketch showing how I and another spy managed to obtain drawings of a fort absolutely under the eyes of a sentry. The spy on the right of the picture is doing nothing more than attracting the attention of the sentry while on the left of the picture I am making the necessary drawings.

It was late that night when we met in the "dodger's" bedroom, and we made complete tracings and finished drawings, each of us taking his own copy for his own headquarters. A day or two later we took steamer together for Malta, where we were to part on our respective homeward journeys—he on his way back to Italy.

As we both had a day or two to wait at Malta, I acted as host to him during his stay. As we entered the harbour I pointed out to him the big 110-ton guns which at that time protected the entrance, and were visible to anybody with two eyes in his head. I pointed out various other interesting batteries to him which were equally obvious, but I omitted to mention other parts which would have been of greater interest to him.

He came away from Malta, however, with the idea that, on the whole, he had done a good stroke of business for his Government by going there, and convinced of his luck in getting hold of a fairly simple thing in the shape of myself to show him around.

It was my good fortune to meet him a few years later, when perhaps unwittingly he returned the compliment which I had done him in Malta. He was then in charge of a large arsenal in one of the colonies of his country. This was situated in a citadel perched on a high ridge with a rapid river flowing around the base.

My orders at that time were to try and ascertain whether any organisation existed in this colony for mobilising the natives as a reserve, should the regular troops be called away for action elsewhere. Also whether there was any means arranged for arming these natives; if so, in what way and in what numbers.

Knowing that my friend was quartered in the place, I called upon him as the first step, without any definite plan in my mind as to how I was to set about getting the information. He was kind enough to take me for a tour of inspection round the town, down to the river, and up in the citadel.

By a lucky chance I got on to the idea that the citadel ought to be lit with electric light since the water power produced by the torrent below could work a dynamo at very low cost if properly engineered. This was so much in my thoughts that as we went through the barracks and buildings in the fort, I kept pointing out how easily and inexpensively places might be wired and lit. And I gradually persuaded him that it was a matter that he should take up and suggest to his superior.

Finally, when he had seen almost everything, my friend remarked: "I don't suppose you would care to see inside the arsenal, it is so much like many others you must have seen before." But I assured him that it would interest me very much; in fact, it was rather essential to forming any approximate estimate for the lighting; and so he took me in.

There was gallery after gallery filled with racks of arms, all beautifully kept, and over the door of each room was the name of the tribe and the number of men who could be mobilised in the event of their being required, and the number of arms and the amount of ammunition that was available for each.

After taking me through two or three rooms, he said: "There are many more like this, but you have probably seen enough." But I eagerly exclaimed that I must see the others in order to judge of this electric lighting scheme. If there were many more rooms it might necessitate an extra sized dynamo, therefore a greater expense, but I hoped that by due economy in the number of lamps to be able to keep down to the original estimate which I had thought of.

So we went steadily through all the rooms, looking at the places where lamps might be most economically established, and I made calculations with pencil and paper, which I showed him, while I jotted on my shirt cuff the names of the tribes and the other information required by my superiors at home—which I did not show him.

The armament of native auxiliaries and their organisation and numbers were thus comparatively easily found out—thanks to that little stroke of luck which I repeat so often comes in to give success whether in scouting or spying.

But a more difficult job was to ascertain the practical fighting value of such people.

TEA AND A TURK

Reports had got about that some wonderful new guns had been installed in one of the forts on the Bosphorus and that a great deal of secrecy was observed in their being put up. It became my duty to go and find out any particulars about them.

My first day in Constantinople was spent under the guidance of an American lady in seeing the sights of the city, and when we had visited almost all the usual resorts for tourists she asked whether there was anything else that I wanted to see, and to a certain extent I let her into my confidence when I told her that I would give anything to see the inside of one of these forts, if it were possible.

She at once said she would be delighted to take me to see her old friend Hamid Pasha, who was quartered in one of them and was always willing to give her and her friends a cup of tea.

When we arrived at the gate of the fort the sentry and the officer in charge would on no account allow us to pass until the lady said that she was a friend of the Pasha, when we were at once admitted and passed to his quarters.

He was a charming host, and received us with the greatest kindness, and after showing us his own quarters and the many curiosities he had collected he took us all round the fort and pointed out its ancient and modern devices for defence, and finally showed us its guns. Two of these, in a somewhat prominent position where they could easily be seen from outside, were covered with canvas covers.

My excitement naturally grew intense when I saw these, and I secretly begged the lady to persuade him to allow us to look at them, and he at once acquiesced, thinking I was an American, and, grinning all over his face, said, "These are our very latest development."

I almost trembled as the covers were drawn off, and then I recognised guns, truly of a modern make but not very new nor powerful, and then he gave away the whole secret by saying: "Of course, we are trying to impress a certain power with the idea that we are re-arming our forts, and therefore we are letting it be known that we are keeping these guns a dead secret and covered from view of any spies."

On another occasion it fell to my lot to inspect some of the defences of the Dardanelles, and I found it could best be done from the seaward. This involved my taking passage in an old grain steamer running between Odessa and Liverpool, and my voyage in her was one of the most charming and original that it has been my lot to take.

A tramp steamer loaded down with grain until its cargo is almost running out of the ventilators is—contrary to all expectations—quite a comfortable boat for cruising in. The captain and his wife lived in comfortable cabins amidships under the bridge; the after deck was stocked with pigs and chickens, which fed liberally on the cargo. The captain's good lady was a Scotch woman, and therefore an excellent cook.

Everything was most clean and comfortable, and the captain most thoroughly entered into my various schemes for observing and examining the defences of the coast as we went along.

He allowed me practically to take command of the ship as regards her course and anchoring. From side to side of the Dardanelles we wandered, and when we came abreast of one of the forts that needed study we anchored ship.

Our erratic procedure naturally invited investigation, and when a Government pilot boat put off to enquire our reason for anchoring in a certain bay he came to the conclusion that our steering gear was not in very good order and that we had stopped to repair it.

While the ship was at anchor a boat was lowered and I whiled away the time, nominally in fishing, but really in cruising about close to the forts and fishing for information rather than for fish by observing the different types of the guns employed and sketching their position and the radius of fire allowed to take them by the splay of their embrasures; also we took soundings where necessary and made sketch maps of possible landing places for attacking or other purposes.

SORE FEET

Bosnia and Herzegovina were under Austrian protection and were supplying a new contingent of infantry to the Austrian army. This force was said to have most marvellous powers of marching and endurance, something hitherto unheard of among European nations. I was told off to ascertain how great these powers might be and what was the secret of their success.

I visited them in their own country. But before I arrived there I had passed through Montenegro, and I had there received reports from Montenegrins, which to some extent discounted the high praise given to them. When I asked a Montenegrin his opinion of his neighbours in the matter of marching and hill climbing, he could only contemptuously spit. And then he explained to me that any fool can go uphill, but a Montenegrin is the only man who can go downhill.

He pointed to the round tower in Cettinje, and told me within it lay several piles of Turks' head, for the reason that every Montenegrin who could show a heap of nine Turks' heads gathered by himself was entitled to a gold medal from the Prince.

Their method of gaining Turks' heads was this:

A party of them would make a raid into Turkish territory and get a few cattle or women. They would then be pursued by the Turks into the mountains, and they would make their way hurriedly up the mountain side just sufficiently far ahead to lead the Turks on to pursue them eagerly. When the Turks had become well strung out in the pursuit, the Montenegrins would suddenly turn on them and charge down the mountain side.

There was no escape for the Turks. They were only ordinary mortals, and could not run downhill. And he showed me his great bare knee, and slapping it with pride, he said: "That is what takes you downhill, and no other nation has a knee like the Montenegrins. And as for the Bosnians—" then he spat!

However, as the Bosnians were reported to be doing such great things in the marching line for the Austrian army, my next step was to visit the Austrian manoeuvres and watch them.

It is usual for a military attaché to be sent officially to watch such manoeuvres, and he is the guest of the Government concerned. But in that position, it is very difficult for him to see behind the scenes. He is only shown what they want him to see. My duty was to go behind the scenes as much as possible and get other points of view.

I accordingly attached myself to a squad of infantry, with whom I spent a couple of days and nights. I had come to a certain town, and could find no room in the place where I could sleep. The hotels were crammed, and even in the shops men were billeted to sleep on and under the counters, as also in every garret and archway in the place.

Finally, I went to the station and asked the stationmaster if I could sleep in a railway carriage. He informed me that all these were filled with troops; but one of the railway men who came from the signal-box a short way down the line took pity on me, and told me if I liked there was his cabin, which I could share with his brother, who was a corporal, and his squad of men, and that I might find room to lie down there.

I gladly climbed the steps into the signal-box, and was made welcome by the corporal and his men in sharing their supplies, and after supper and a chat I bedded down amongst them.

It was interesting to see how conscientiously this little party did its work. At every hour during the night the corporal went out and inspected his sentry, just as if on active service, and patrols were frequent and reports handed in, although no officer ever came near the place.

During the next two days we had plenty of experience of marching and counter-marching, firing and charging; but going along in the rear of the immense mass of troops one soon realised what enormous wastage there is in stragglers, and especially those with sore feet. So much so was this the case that wagons came along, picked up the sore-footed men, and carried them back to the railway, where every evening a special train was in attendance to convey them back to their garrison.

A few that were missed out by this operation on the field were collected into their field hospitals, and thus the numbers shown every day to the general staff of men admitted to hospital for sore feet was very small indeed compared with the number that were actually put out of action from that cause.

It was soon quite evident that my friend the Montenegrin had not spat without reason, and that the Bosnians were no harder in their feet than the other nationalities in that variegated army.

AUSTRIAN OFFICERS

I had a very strong fellow feeling for the Austrian army and its officers. They were so very much like our own, but far more amateurish in their knowledge and methods of leading; as old-fashioned as the hills, and liable to make mistakes at every turn.

The only one who seemed to realise this was the aged Emperor himself, and when he came flying along it was very like the Duke of Cambridge at his best with a thunderstorm raging.

The army was then commanded by Arch-Dukes, aged men as a rule, and all intensely nervous as to what the Emperor would think of them when he came along. One could tell when he was coming by watching the feathers in their helmets. An Arch-Duke would look very brave in all his war paint, but if you watched the green feather above him closely you might notice it trembling with a distinct shiver when the Emperor was anywhere in the neighbourhood.

Their old-fashioned methods and amateurish leading seem to be paying a heavy price in the present campaign.

AN INTERESTING TASK

A new method of illuminating the battlefield at night had been invented on the Continent.

A chemical substance had been manufactured which enabled the user to turn on a strong light over a wide space at any moment.

Rumour said that it was as powerful as a searchlight, and yet could be carried in your pocket. But great secrecy was observed both regarding its composition and its experimental trials.

In the same army a new kind of observation balloon was said to be on trial equipped with some very up-to-date apparatus.

Also it was reported that, in addition to these aids to effective reconnaissance, a new method of swimming rivers by cavalry had been invented by which every man and horse in a cavalry division could cross wide rivers without difficulty or delay.

Owing to political strain going on in Europe at the time there was the possibility that these rumours might have been purposely set on foot, like many others, with a view to giving some moral prestige to the army concerned.

It became my duty to investigate as far as possible what amount of truth lay in them.

ENCOUNTER WITH THE POLICE

It was a difficult country to work in owing to the very stringent police arrangements against spies of every kind, and it looked to be a most unpromising task to elicit what I wanted to know, because one was sure of being watched at every turn. As I afterwards discovered, it was through this multiplicity of police arrangements that one was able to get about with comparative ease, because if one went boldly enough it immediately argued to the watchful policeman that someone else was sure to be observing you.

Moreover, spies generally do their work single-handed, and on this occasion I was accompanied by my brother, and this made it easier for us to go about as a pair of tourists interested in the country generally. A man travelling alone is much more liable to draw attention upon himself, and therefore to go about under suspicion.

Our entry into the country was not altogether fortunate, because while yet in the train we managed to get into trouble with the guard over a window which he insisted on shutting when we wanted it open. In the same carriage with us was a gentleman of some standing in the country, and in a fit of absent-mindedness I made a little sketch of him. I had just completed it when an arm reached down over my shoulder from behind and the picture was snatched away by the observant guard of the train and taken off to be used as evidence against me.

The guard of a train in this country, I may say, ranks apparently much the same as a colonel in the army, and therefore is not a man to be trifled with. On our arrival at the terminus we found a sort of guard of honour of gendarmes waiting for us on the platform, and we were promptly marched off to the police office to account for our procedure in the train by daring to open the window when the guard wished it closed, and for drawing caricatures of a "high-born" man in the train.

We made no secret as to our identity and handed our cards to the commissary of police when we were brought up before him. He was—till that moment—glaring at us fiercely, evidently deciding what punishment to give us before he had heard our case at all. But when he saw my brother's name as an officer in the Guards, he asked: "Does this mean in the Guards of her Majesty Queen

Victoria?" When he heard it was so his whole demeanour changed. He sprang from his seat, begged us to be seated, and explained it was all a mistake. Evidently Guards in his country were in very high repute. He explained to us there were certain little irritating rules on the railway which had to be enforced, but, of course, in our case we were not to be bound by such small bye-laws, and with profuse apologies he bowed us out of the office, without a stain upon our characters.

SUCCESS WITH THE BALLOON

We did not live long without the stain. Our first anxiety was to find where and how it would be possible to see some of this equipment for which we had come to the country. Manoeuvres were going on at a place some fifty miles distant, and there, as tourists, we betook ourselves without delay. We put up at a small inn not far from the railway-station, and for the next few days we did immense walking tours, following up the troops and watching them at their work over a very extended area of country.

At last one day we sighted a balloon hanging in the sky, and we made a bee line for it until we arrived at its station. When it was hauled down and anchored to the ground the men went off to the camp to get their dinners, and the balloon was left without a soul to guard it. It was not long before we were both inside the car, taking note of everything in the shape of the instruments and their makers' names, and so had all the information it was possible to get before the men came back.

HOW TO ENTER A FORT

Our next step was to see this wonderful illuminant for night work, and in the course of our wandering's we came across a large fort from which searchlights had been showing the previous night. There were notice boards round this fort at a distance of about twenty yards apart stating that nobody was allowed within this circle of notices, and we argued that if once we were inside any sentry or detective would naturally suppose we had leave to be there.

We tried the idea, and it worked splendidly. We walked calmly through camps and past sentries without a tremor and not a question was asked us. Once within this line we were able to get directly into the fort, and there we strolled along as if the place belonged to us.

There is a certain amount of art required in making yourself not appear to be a stranger in a new place.

In the minor matter of hat, boots, and necktie it is well to wear those bought in the country you are visiting, otherwise your British-made articles are sure to attract the attention of a watchful policeman.

In the matter of demeanour you behave as a native would do who was accustomed to being there.

Walking into a strange fort must be carried out much on the same lines as you would adopt in entering a strange town, only more so. You walk as if with a set purpose to get to a certain part of it, as though you knew the way perfectly, and without showing any kind of interest in what is around you. If you pass an officer or dignitary whom you see everybody saluting, salute him too, so that you do not appear singular. When you want to observe any special feature you loaf about reading a newspaper or, if in a town, by looking at all you want to see as reflected in a shop window.

The penalty for spying in this country was five years without the option of a fine, or even of a trial.

Having walked in like this, and having successfully walked out again—which is quite another matter—we felt elated with our success and hung about till nightfall and tried it again after dark. This was no easy job, as the place was surrounded by outposts very much on the *qui vive* for an enemy that was to make a manoeuvre attack during the night. By keeping to leeward of the general position one was able to quietly creep along, sniffing the breeze, until one could judge where there was an outpost and where there was open ground, and in this manner, smelling our way as we went, we were able to creep through between the outposts and so gained the fort.

HOW WE GOT THE SECRET LIGHT

This time it meant slipping through unperceived as far as possible, and in this we succeeded equally well. By good fortune we arrived just before experiments commenced with the illuminating rockets. Everybody's attention was centred on these and no one had time to notice or observe what we were doing. We watched the preparations and also the results, and having studied the routine and the geography of the practice we were in the end able to help ourselves to some of the rockets and the lighting composition, and with these we eventually made off. Without delay we placed our treasures in the hands of a trusty agent who transferred them at once to England.

HOW THE BIG RIVER WAS SWUM

Our next step was to see how crossing the river was carried out by the cavalry. From information received we presented ourselves at a certain spot on the river at a little before ten one morning. The official attachés had received notice that a brigade of cavalry would swim the river at this point at ten o'clock, and at ten o'clock their special train was due to arrive there.

We were there, fortunately, half an hour beforehand, and we saw the whole brigade come down to the river and file across a fairly deep ford, where the horses got wet to some extent, but they did not swim.

On the far bank a few men were left behind. These, as it turned out, were all the men and horses who could actually swim well, and as the train arrived and the attachés disembarked on to the bank they found the major part of the brigade already arrived, dripping wet, and the remainder just swimming over at that moment.

Of course in their reports they stated that they had seen the whole brigade swimming over. But this is how reports very often get about which are not strictly true.

CAUGHT AT LAST

Emboldened by our success in getting into the fort by day and night, we then continued the experiment for several nights in succession, watching the further practice with searchlights, star shells, and light rockets. We had, however, collected all the information that was necessary, and there was no need for us to go there again. But news reached us that there was to be a final show for the Emperor himself, and I could not resist the temptation of going once more to the fort, as I expected there would be a grand pyrotechnic display for this occasion.

I got there in good time before the Emperor's arrival, and made my way into the place as usual, my brother remaining outside to see the effect of the lights from the attacker's point of view. Inside, however, all was not quite the same as it had been on previous occasions. There were a very large number of officers collected there, and a too larger number of police, officers for my liking. I, therefore, repented of my intention and took myself out again.

Then as I walked back along the road in the dark I noticed the lights of the Emperor's *cortege* coming along towards me. As the first carriage passed me I did the worst thing in the world I could have done at such a moment—I turned my head away to avoid being recognised in the lamplight. My action made the occupants of the first carriage suspicious. They were some of the staff officers of the Emperor.

In a moment they stopped the carriage, rushed at me, and with scarcely a word, seized and hustled me into the carriage with them, and drove back to the fort again. They asked me a few questions as to who I was and why I was there, and on arrival at the fort I was handed over to some other officers and again asked my business.

I could only say that I was an Englishman who had been looking on at the manoeuvres as a spectator and was anxious to find my way to the station (which was some ten miles away). This was all fairly true, but not quite good enough for them, and they presently packed me into a carriage and sent me back—in charge of an officer—to the station, with a view to my being handed over to the police and removed to the capital.

It was in the days of my apprenticeship, and I had been exceedingly foolish in taking a few notes, which, although undecipherable, perhaps would none the less be used as evidence against me.

Therefore, so soon as we were under way I made it my business to quietly tear these notes up into small pieces, and to drop them out of the carriage window whenever my guardian was looking the other way. When we arrived at the station there was some little time to wait, and I asked if I might go to the inn and collect my belongings. Permission was granted to me, and I was taken there under the charge of a police officer.

Hastily I packed my bag, and the good officer endeavoured to help me, packing up anything he could see in the room and thrusting it in with my things. Unfortunately he kept packing my brother's things in as well, and so when his back was turned I thrust them back into my brother's bed, for I did not want it known he was about there too.

Having finally filled my portmanteau, my next care was to leave a warning lest he too should be entrapped. So while ostensibly paying the bill to the landlord of the house, who had been called up by the police, I wrote a warning note on a scrap of paper, which I jammed on the candle, where my brother could not fail to find it when he came home later on, and then I went off to the station, and was taken back to the capital by a Hussar officer of congenial temperament.

With all good feeling and the true hospitality of his kind, he insisted on buying half a dozen bottles of beer for my consumption—since I was an Englishman—and he helped me with the ordeal during the small hours of the morning.

On reaching the capital I was put into a hotel, my passport taken from me, and I was told that I should be expected to remain there until called for. In the meantime I might go about the city, but was not to take myself away without permission. I very soon found that I was being watched by a detective told off for the purpose, and then it was that I made the acquaintance of a foreign spy who was acting as waiter in the hotel. He was so well informed on higher politics, as well as on military matters, that I guessed he must be an officer of the intelligence staff, and he was most helpful and kind to me in my predicament.

He pointed out to me who were the detectives in the hotel staff, and informed me that their duty was merely to watch me, to ascertain what my moves were day by day, and to report them by telephone to the head police office. He advised me before going out each day to inform the hall porter, thereby letting the detectives overhear what were my plans; they would then telephone to the police, who would have their own detectives watching me while I was out.

THE ESCAPE

Within a short time my brother rejoined me from the manoeuvre area, but by doing so he at once came under observation and under suspicion, and we were practically a pair of prisoners. So much was this the case that a few days later we received a visit at daybreak one morning, from a friend in power, who was also in touch with the police, and he advised us that the best course we could take was to escape from the country while it was possible, he undertaking quietly to make arrangements for us. The idea was that we should slip away to a seaport, where we could get on to a British steamer as two of the crew and so pass out of the country.

That was the scheme. But the difficulty was how to play it off. A ship was found whose captain was willing to receive us provided that we could get to him without being observed. With the aid of our friendly waiter, we let the detective at the hotel understand that we were tired of being under suspicion, and that we were boldly going to take the train and leave the country.

At ten o'clock a cab was to come round to take us and our luggage to the station, and if anybody interfered with us—why, we were freeborn British, and subject to no man's rule, and the Ambassador and all the rest of the Powers should hear about it! This was for the information of the detective, and he merely telephoned it to the police office at the railway station, where we should be arrested at the point of our departure.

We got into our cab and drove off down the street towards the station until we were out of sight of the hotel. Then we called to our driver and said we should like to go to a different station. This course involved our going to the river-side and taking the ferry.

It was an anxious time. Had we been spotted? Should we be missed? Were we being followed?

These questions would answer themselves as we progressed with our plot. The answer, when it came, would mean a tremendous lot to us—triumph or five years' imprisonment; so we had every right to be fairly anxious. And yet, somehow, I don't think we were worrying much about the consequences, but rather were busy with the present—as to how to evade pursuit and recapture.

Arrived at the ferry we paid off our cabman and made our way to the quay-side. Here we found a boat which had already been arranged for; and we made our way safely off to the ship, which was waiting under steam in midstream to start the moment we were on board.

At this supreme moment my brother had the temerity to argue with the boatman over the fare. Being now in the last stage of tender-hooks, I adjured him to give the man double what he asked, if only to be free. But the brother was calm, and for once—he was right! His display of want of all anxiety quite diverted any kind of suspicion that might have attached to us, and in the end we got safely on board and away.

CONCLUSION

Such are some of the minor experiences which, though not very sensational in themselves, are yet part of the every-day work of an "intelligence agent" (*alias* a spy), and while they tend to relieve such work of any suspicion of monotony, they add, as a rule, that touch of romance and excitement to it which makes spying the fascinating sport that it is.

When one recognises also that it may have invaluable results for one's country in time of war, one feels that even though it is a time spent largely in enjoyment, it is not by any means time thrown idly away; and though the "agent," if caught, may "go under," unhonoured and unsung, he knows in his heart of hearts that he has done as bravely for his country as his comrade who falls in battle.

Lightning Source UK Ltd.
Milton Keynes UK
UKHW010509241019
352206UK00002B/307/P